CSS Flexbox Layout

Abdelfattah Ragab

CSS Flexbox Layout

Abdelfattah Ragab

Introduction

Welcome to "CSS Flexbox Layout". In this book I explain the flexbox layout model. I explain the properties of containers and elements and show you how to use Flexbox to create modern and responsive web designs. By the end of this book, you will know everything about Flexbox, use it to create responsive designs and handle all kinds of scenarios.
Let's get started.

Key concepts

CSS3 Flexbox, also known as Flexible Box Layout, is a powerful layout model that allows you to create flexible and responsive layouts for web pages. It provides a straightforward way to arrange and distribute elements within a container, even when the container's size or the elements' dimensions vary.

To use Flexbox, you need to set the parent element (the flex container) to display: flex or display: inline-flex. This enables the Flexbox behavior for the container and establishes a flex formatting context. Here are some key concepts and properties used in Flexbox:

Flex Container Properties

- `display`: flex or display: inline-flex: Specifies that the container is a flex container and its children are flex items.
- `flex-direction`: Defines the direction of the main axis, which determines how flex items are positioned. Values can be row, row-reverse, column, or column-reverse.
- `justify-content`: Aligns flex items along the main axis. It controls the spacing between and

around the flex items. Values include flex-start, flex-end, center, space-between, space-around, and space-evenly.

- `align-items`: Aligns flex items along the cross axis (perpendicular to the main axis). It controls how flex items are distributed vertically. Values can be flex-start, flex-end, center, baseline, or stretch.
- `flex-wrap`: Specifies whether flex items should wrap to multiple lines when they exceed the width of the flex container. Values include nowrap, wrap, and wrap-reverse.
- `align-content`: Defines the alignment of flex lines when there is extra space on the cross axis. It applies to multi-line flex containers. Values can be flex-start, flex-end, center, space-between, space-around, or stretch.

Flex Item Properties

- `flex-grow`: Specifies the ability of a flex item to grow to fill available space. It determines how the remaining space is distributed among flex items. Default value is 0.

- `flex-shrink:` Specifies the ability of a flex item to shrink if necessary when the flex container is too small. Default value is 1.
- `flex-basis:` Specifies the initial size of a flex item before it's distributed in the flex container. Values can be a length, a percentage, or auto.
- `flex:` Shorthand for flex-grow, flex-shrink, and flex-basis.
- `order:` Defines the order in which flex items are displayed. Lower values appear first. Default value is 0.

Alignment of Individual Flex Items

- `align-self:` Overrides the align-items property for a specific flex item. It allows you to align an item along the cross axis independently. Values can be auto, flex-start, flex-end, center, baseline, or stretch.

Flexbox provides much more flexibility and additional properties than the ones mentioned above. By leveraging these properties, you can create complex and responsive layouts with ease. Experimenting and combining different Flexbox properties will help you achieve the desired layout for your web page.

We have 5 div elements with different sizes and colors as follows. By setting display flex on their wrapper, they will be displayed as follows.

```
<style>
  .wrapper {
    display: flex;
  }
  .div-1 {
    width: 100px;
    height: 160px;
    background-color: magenta;
  }
  .div-2 {
    width: 60px;
    height: 170px;
    background-color: blue;
  }
```

```css
  .div-3 {
    width: 100px;
    height: 180px;
    background-color: green;
  }
  .div-4 {
    width: 100px;
    height: 120px;
    background-color: brown;
  }
  .div-5 {
    width: 120px;
    height: 160px;
    background-color: orange;
  }
</style>
<div class="wrapper">
  <div class="div-1"></div>
  <div class="div-2"></div>
  <div class="div-3"></div>
  <div class="div-4"></div>
  <div class="div-5"></div>
</div>
```

Before applying display flex to the wrapper, they looked
like this

Now let's understand how flex layout works.

Flex layout has two main axes, the main axis and the cross axis

The main axis is defined by the flex-direction property, and the cross axis runs perpendicular to it.

flex-direction can have four values: row, column, row-reverse, and column-reverse.

flex-direction, if not specified, is set to row by default

flex-direction

The flex-direction property specifies the direction of the flexible elements.

If the element is not a flexible element, the flex-direction property has no effect.

Values

- row
- row-reverse
- column
- column-reverse

row

Default value. The flexible items are displayed horizontally, as a row

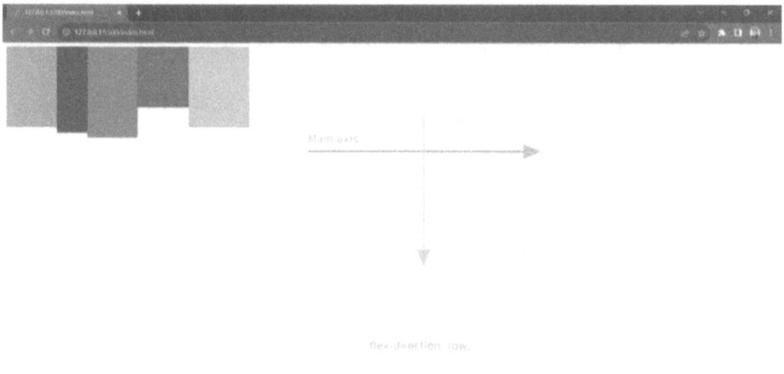

```
.wrapper {
  display: flex;
  flex-direction: row;
```

```
}
```

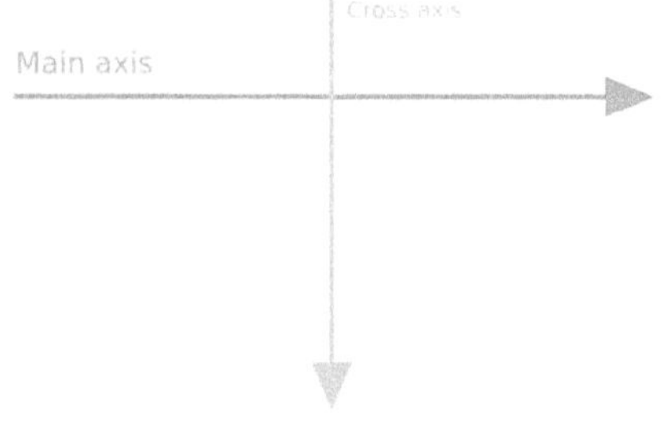

row-reverse

Same as row, but in reverse order

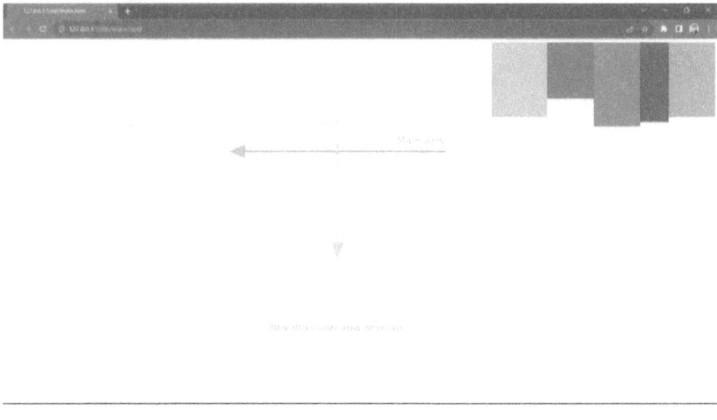


```
.wrapper {
  display: flex;
```

```
    flex-direction: row-reverse;
}
```

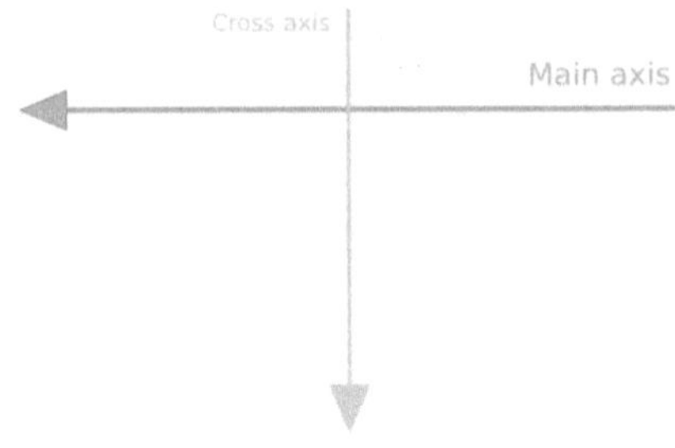

column

The flexible items are displayed vertically, as a column

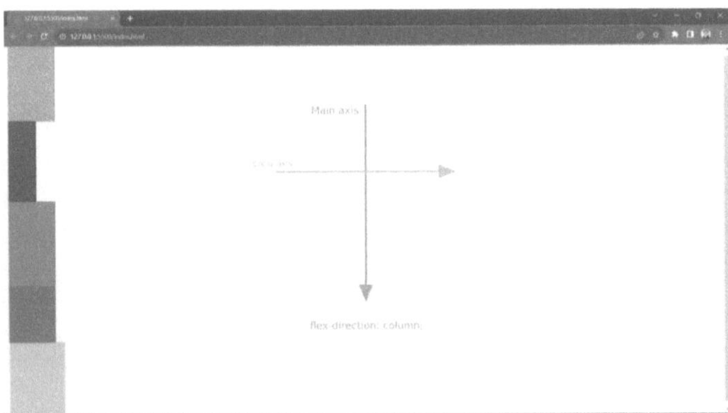


```
.wrapper {
```

```css
    display: flex;
    flex-direction: column;
}
```

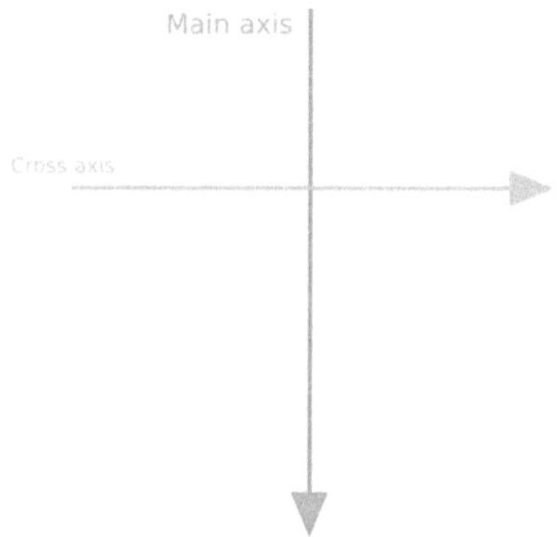

column-reverse

Same as column, but in reverse order

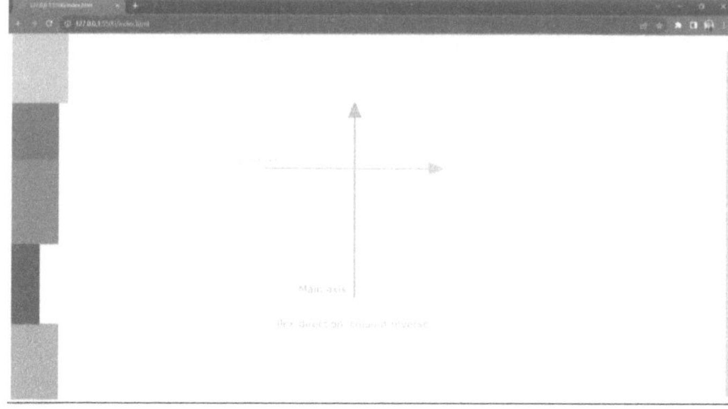

```css
.wrapper {
  display: flex;
  flex-direction: column-reverse;
}
```

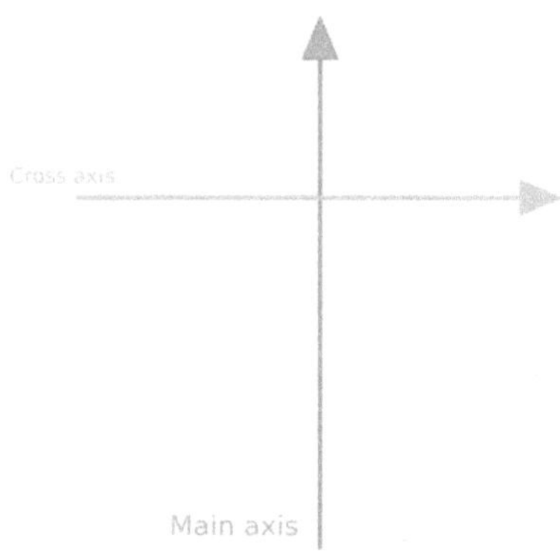

Now let's look at how you can benefit from this, starting with two important flex layout properties justify-content and align-items.

I will explain the flex direction of the row in detail and leave it to you to try the other flex directions

justify-content

The CSS property justify-content determines how the browser distributes the space between and around content elements along the main axis of a flex container

Values

- flex-start
- flex-end
- center
- space-between
- space-around
- space-evenly

Let's explain each value and see it in action

I'll start with the default value, flex-start

flex-start

Default value. Items are positioned at the beginning of the container

```
.wrapper {
  display: flex;
  flex-direction: row;
  justify-content: flex-start;
}
```

flex-end

Items are positioned at the end of the container

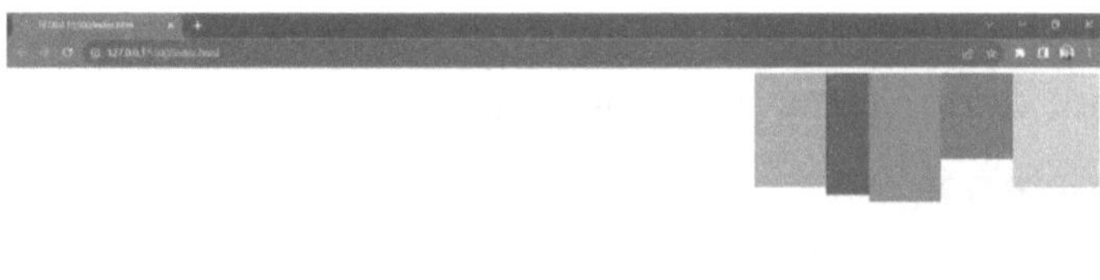

```css
.wrapper {
  display: flex;
  flex-direction: row;
  justify-content: flex-end;
}
```

It is aligned at the end of the flex container to the right of the screen. You must note that there is a difference between flex-direction: row-reversed and justify-content: flex-end;

They are not the same thing. Justify-content is about alignment, i.e. it keeps the same order and aligns it to the end of the flex container. In the case of flex-direction: row-reverse, the main axis is reversed and so is the order.

center

Items are positioned in the center of the container

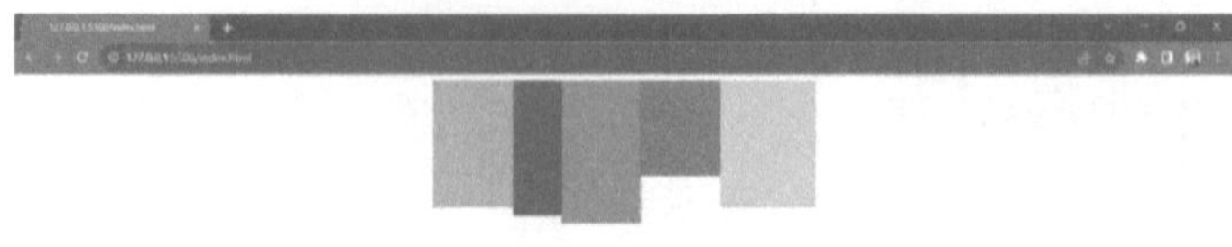

```css
.wrapper {
  display: flex;
  flex-direction: row;
  justify-content: center;
}
```

space-between

Items will have space between them

```css
.wrapper {
  display: flex;
  flex-direction: row;
  justify-content: space-between;
}
```

space-around

Items will have space before, between, and after them

```css
.wrapper {
  display: flex;
  flex-direction: row;
  justify-content: space-around;
}
```

space-evenly

Items will have equal space around them

```css
.wrapper {
  display: flex;
  flex-direction: row;
  justify-content: space-evenly;
}
```

That was for the main axis, now let's see how we can align the elements on the cross axis with the align-items property

align-items

Controls the alignment of items on the Cross Axis.

Values

- normal
- stretch
- center

- flex-start
- flex-end
- baseline

Let's explain each value and see it in action

I'll start with the default value, normal or stretch

normal or stretch (same behavior)

Items are stretched to fit the container

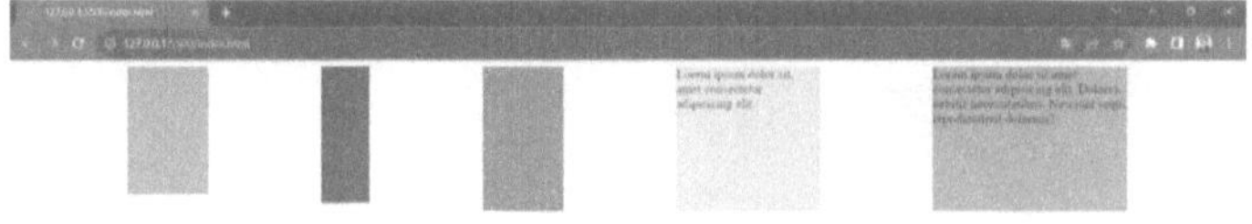

```
<style>
  .wrapper {
    display: flex;
    flex-direction: row;
    justify-content: space-evenly;
    align-items: stretch;
  }
  .div-1 {
```

```css
    width: 100px;
    height: 160px;
    background-color: magenta;
  }
  .div-2 {
    width: 60px;
    height: 170px;
    background-color: blue;
  }

  .div-3 {
    width: 100px;
    height: 180px;
    background-color: green;
  }
  .div-4 {
    width: 180px;
    height: auto;
    background-color: mediumspringgreen;
  }
  .div-5 {
    width: 240px;
    height: auto;
    background-color: orangered;
  }
</style>
```

```html
<div class="wrapper">
  <div class="div-1"></div>
  <div class="div-2"></div>
  <div class="div-3"></div>
  <div class="div-4">
    Lorem ipsum dolor sit, amet consectetur
adipisicing elit.
  </div>
  <div class="div-5">
    Lorem ipsum dolor sit amet consectetur
adipisicing elit. Dolores, debitis
    necessitatibus. Nesciunt sequi
reprehenderit dolorum?
  </div>
</div>
```

The last two div elements now expand to fill the entire height of the container

center

Items are positioned at the center of the container

```css
.wrapper {
  display: flex;
  flex-direction: row;
  justify-content: space-evenly;
  align-items: center;
}
```

flex-start

Items are positioned at the beginning of the container

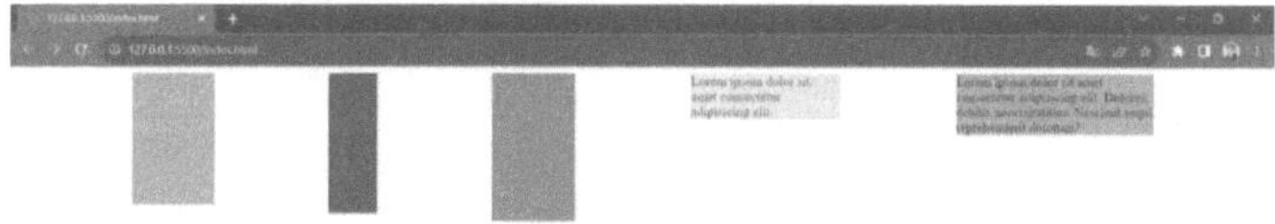

```css
.wrapper {
  display: flex;
  flex-direction: row;
  justify-content: space-evenly;
  align-items: flex-start;
}
```

flex-end

Items are positioned at the end of the container

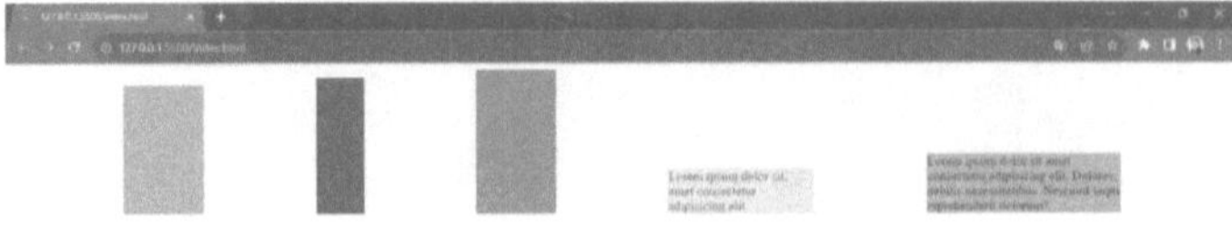

```
.wrapper {
  display: flex;
  flex-direction: row;
  justify-content: space-evenly;
  align-items: flex-end;
}
```

baseline

Items are positioned at the baseline of the container

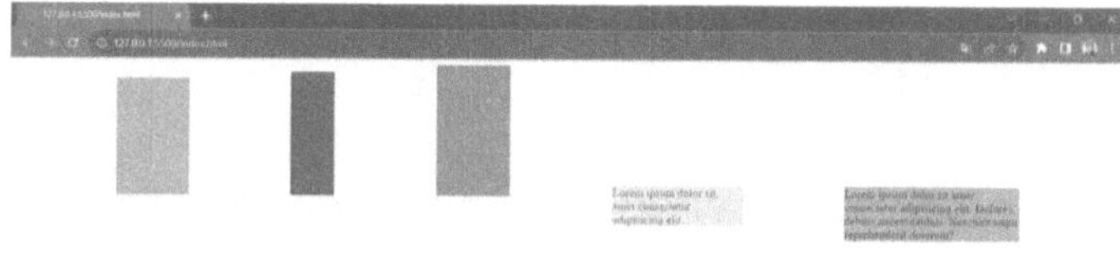

```css
.wrapper {
  display: flex;
  flex-direction: row;
  justify-content: space-evenly;
  align-items: baseline;
}
```

Have you considered what happens when we have many div elements that exceed the width of the container?

There is a flex property that handles this case. It is called flex-wrap

flex-wrap

The CSS property flex-wrap determines whether flex elements are forced into one line or can wrap into multiple lines.

To better understand this, I want to increase the number of div elements on the page so that they no longer fit on one line.

Values

- nowrap
- wrap
- wrap-reverse

nowrap

Default value. Specifies that the flexible items will not wrap

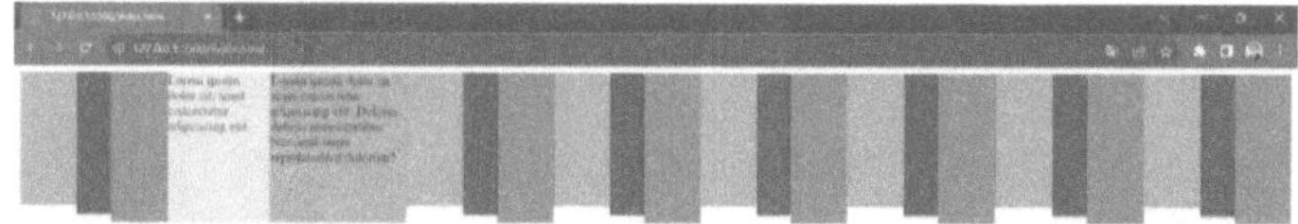

```
<style>
  .wrapper {
    display: flex;
    flex-direction: row;
    flex-wrap: nowrap;
  }
  .div-1 {
    width: 100px;
    height: 160px;
    background-color: magenta;
  }
  .div-2 {
    width: 60px;
    height: 170px;
    background-color: blue;
  }
```

```
    .div-3 {
      width: 100px;
      height: 180px;
      background-color: green;
    }
    .div-4 {
      width: 180px;
      height: auto;
      background-color: mediumspringgreen;
    }
    .div-5 {
      width: 240px;
      height: auto;
      background-color: orangered;
    }
</style>
<div class="wrapper">
  <div class="div-1"></div>
  <div class="div-2"></div>
  <div class="div-3"></div>
  <div class="div-4">
    Lorem ipsum dolor sit, amet consectetur
adipisicing elit.
  </div>
  <div class="div-5">
```

```html
      Lorem ipsum dolor sit amet consectetur
adipisicing elit. Dolores, debitis
      necessitatibus. Nesciunt sequi
reprehenderit dolorum?
    </div>
    <div class="div-1"></div>
    <div class="div-2"></div>
    <div class="div-3"></div>
    <div class="div-1"></div>
    <div class="div-2"></div>
    <div class="div-3"></div>
    <div class="div-1"></div>
    <div class="div-2"></div>
    <div class="div-3"></div>
    <div class="div-1"></div>
    <div class="div-2"></div>
    <div class="div-3"></div>
    <div class="div-1"></div>
    <div class="div-2"></div>
    <div class="div-3"></div>
    <div class="div-1"></div>
    <div class="div-2"></div>
    <div class="div-3"></div>
  </div>
```

The div elements have been shrunk to fit the width of
the container. This happens because of the flex property

flex-shrink, which has a default value of 1, which means that the elements should be shrunk to fit into the container.

I will disable this property for now to see the actual behavior of the elements without flex-shrink. Deactivate it by setting the value to 0;

flex-shrink is a property for the flex element and not for the flex container, i.e. it must be set for each flex element in the flex container.

In the flex layout, we have the flex container that we have worked with so far and which we have marked with the .wrapper class.

And we have flex elements that are div elements of div-1, div-2,... etc.

We will discuss the flex elements and their properties soon, but first let's understand flex-wrap and now disable flex-shrink for all flex elements

Select all div elements within the .wrapper and deactivate the flex-shrink property

```css
.wrapper div {
  flex-shrink: 0;
}
```

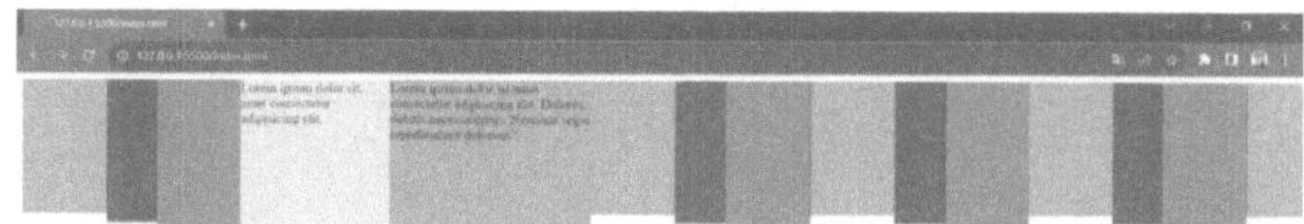

As you can see, the elements have retained their original size, but now we have a scrollbar at the bottom of the page

Specifies that the flexible items will wrap if necessary

Now we will see how the elements within the flex
container are wrapped by setting the flex-wrap property
to the value wrap

```css
.wrapper {
  display: flex;
  flex-direction: row;
  flex-wrap: wrap;
}
```

To make it clearer, I number all div elements

```
<style>
  .wrapper {
    display: flex;
    flex-direction: row;
    flex-wrap: wrap;
  }
  .wrapper div {
    flex-shrink: 0;
  }
  .div-1 {
    width: 100px;
    height: 160px;
    background-color: magenta;
    font-size: 24px;
  }
  .div-2 {
```

```css
    width: 60px;
    height: 170px;
    background-color: blue;
    font-size: 24px;
  }


  .div-3 {
    width: 100px;
    height: 180px;
    background-color: green;
    font-size: 24px;
  }
  .div-4 {
    width: 180px;
    height: auto;
    background-color: mediumspringgreen;
  }
  .div-5 {
    width: 240px;
    height: auto;
    background-color: orangered;
  }
</style>
<div class="wrapper">
  <div class="div-1">1</div>
  <div class="div-2">2</div>
```

```
<div class="div-3">3</div>
<div class="div-4">
    Lorem ipsum dolor sit, amet consectetur
adipisicing elit.
</div>
<div class="div-5">
    Lorem ipsum dolor sit amet consectetur
adipisicing elit. Dolores, debitis
    necessitatibus. Nesciunt sequi
reprehenderit dolorum?
</div>
<div class="div-1">6</div>
<div class="div-2">7</div>
<div class="div-3">8</div>
<div class="div-1">9</div>
<div class="div-2">10</div>
<div class="div-3">11</div>
<div class="div-1">12</div>
<div class="div-2">13</div>
<div class="div-3">14</div>
<div class="div-1">15</div>
<div class="div-2">16</div>
<div class="div-3">17</div>
<div class="div-1">18</div>
<div class="div-2">19</div>
<div class="div-3">20</div>
```

```html
    <div class="div-1">21</div>
    <div class="div-2">22</div>
    <div class="div-3">23</div>
</div>
```

wrap-reverse

Specifies that the flexible elements should be wrapped in reverse order.

```css
.wrapper {
    display: flex;
    flex-direction: row;
    flex-wrap: wrap-reverse;
}
```

gap

The gap property defines the size of the gap between the rows and between the columns in flexbox, grid or multi-column layout. It is a shorthand for the following properties: row-gap and column-gap

Values

- <row-gap> <column-gap>

row-gap column-gap

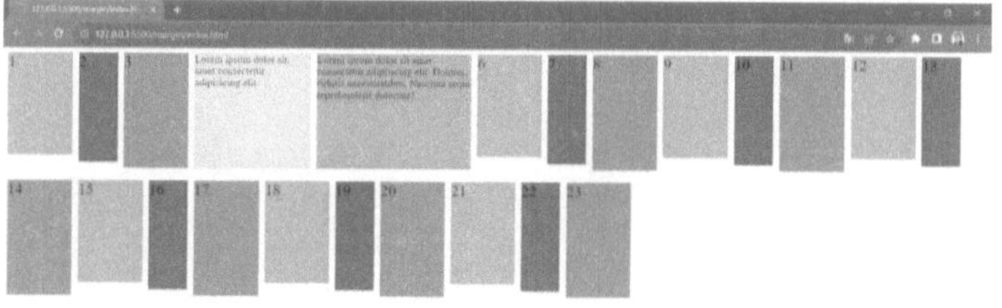

```
.wrapper {
  display: flex;
  flex-direction: row;
  flex-wrap: wrap;
  gap: 20px 10px;
}
```

align-content

The align-content property determines how the flex lines are distributed along the transverse axis in a flexbox container.

It only works if your flex elements extend over several lines and there is therefore a space between the lines.

It has no effect if the elements are only in one line.

Values

- stretch
- center
- flex-start
- flex-end
- space-between
- space-around
- space-evenly

stretch

Default value. Lines stretch to take up the remaining space

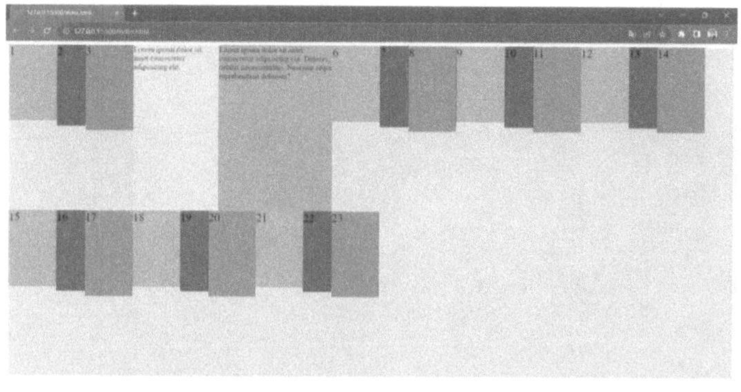

```
.wrapper {
  display: flex;
  flex-direction: row;
  flex-wrap: wrap;
  height: 700px;
  background-color: lightblue;
  align-content: stretch;
}
```

center

Lines are packed toward the center of the flex container

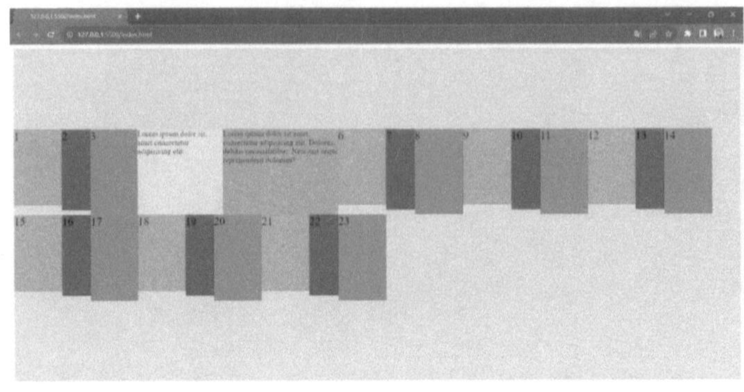

```css
.wrapper {
  display: flex;
  flex-direction: row;
  flex-wrap: wrap;
  height: 700px;
  background-color: lightblue;
  align-content: center;
}
```

flex-start

Lines are packed toward the start of the flex container

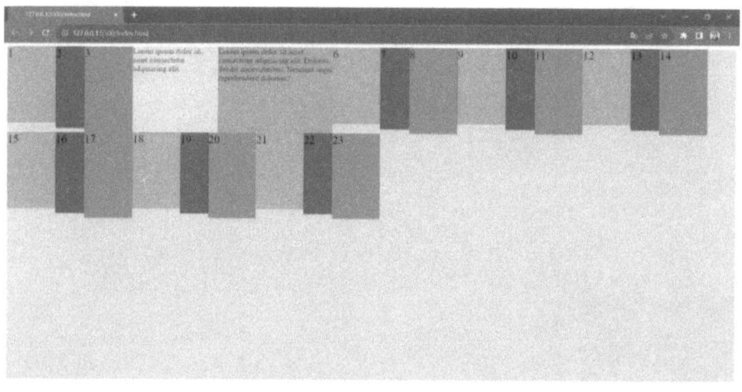

```
.wrapper {
  display: flex;
  flex-direction: row;
  flex-wrap: wrap;
  height: 700px;
  background-color: lightblue;
  align-content: flex-start;
}
```

flex-end

Lines are packed toward the end of the flex container

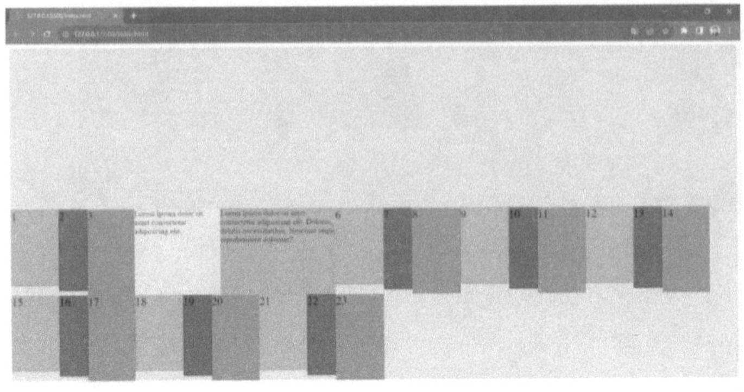

```
.wrapper {
  display: flex;
  flex-direction: row;
  flex-wrap: wrap;
  height: 700px;
  background-color: lightblue;
  align-content: flex-end;
}
```

space-between

Lines are evenly distributed in the flex container

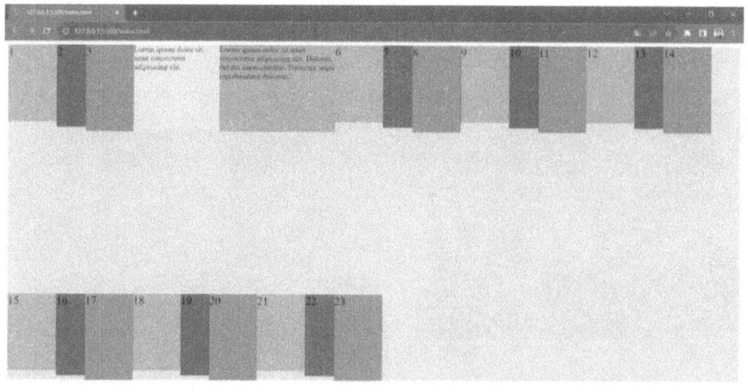

```
.wrapper {
  display: flex;
  flex-direction: row;
  flex-wrap: wrap;
  height: 700px;
  background-color: lightblue;
  align-content: space-between;
}
```

space-around

Lines are evenly distributed in the flex container, with half-size spaces on either end

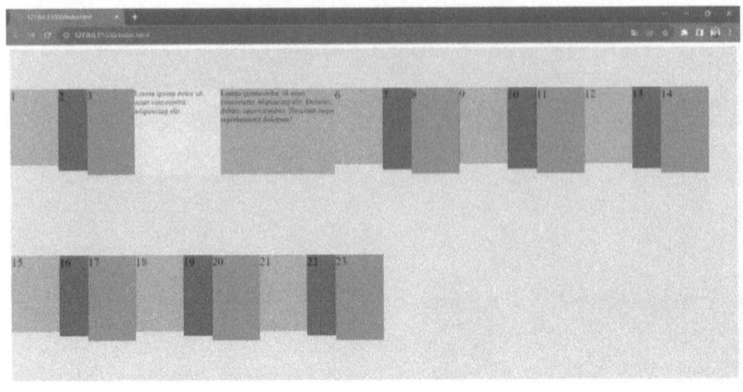

```
.wrapper {
  display: flex;
  flex-direction: row;
  flex-wrap: wrap;
  height: 700px;
  background-color: lightblue;
  align-content: space-around;
}
```

space-evenly

Lines are evenly distributed in the flex container, with equal space around them

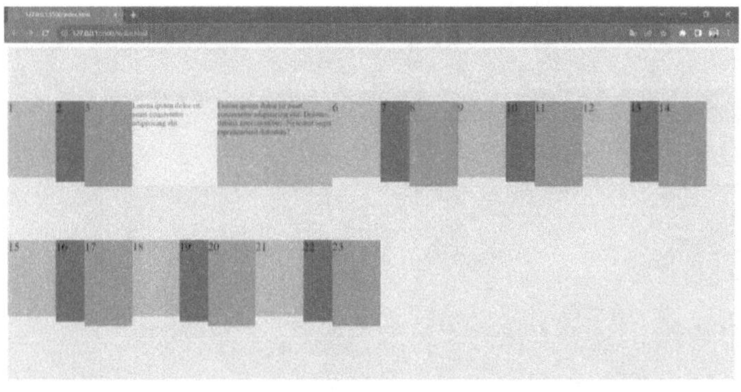

```css
.wrapper {
  display: flex;
  flex-direction: row;
  flex-wrap: wrap;
  height: 700px;
  background-color: lightblue;
  align-content: space-evenly;
}
```

You can combine other properties, such as, row-gap, column-gap, gap, align-items…etc.

column-gap and align-items

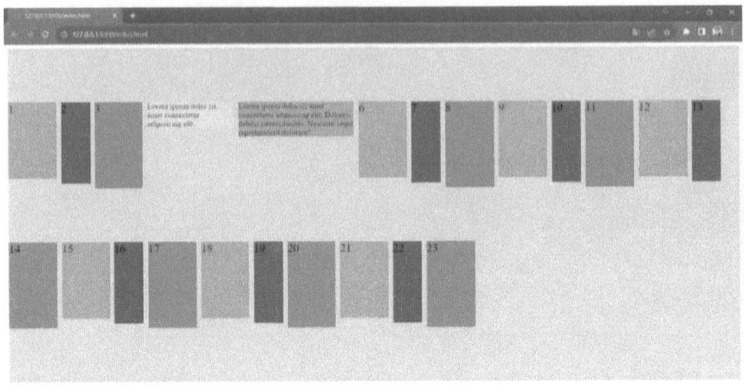

```
.wrapper {
  display: flex;
  flex-direction: row;
  flex-wrap: wrap;
  height: 700px;
  background-color: lightblue;
  align-content: space-evenly;
  column-gap: 10px;
  align-items: flex-start;
}
```

Now that we have looked at the properties of the flex container, let's explain the properties of the flex elements.

Flex Item Properties

The direct subordinate elements of a flex container automatically become flex elements.

In our examples, the .wrapper div element is the flex container and all subordinate div elements such as .div-1, .div-2, ... etc. are the flex elements.
The flex item properties are defined individually for each one

flex-grow

The flex-grow property specifies how much the item will grow relative to the rest of the flexible items inside the same container.

Values

- number

number

I will apply flex-grow to the blue div, .div-2

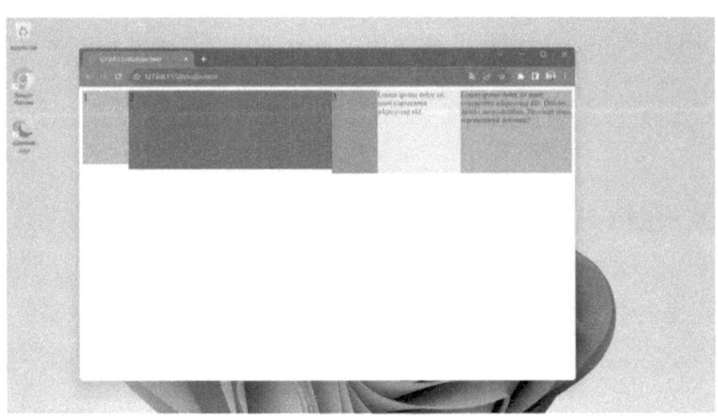

```html
<style>
  .wrapper {
    display: flex;
    flex-direction: row;
    flex-wrap: wrap;
  }
  .div-1 {
    width: 100px;
    height: 160px;
```

```css
    background-color: magenta;
    font-size: 24px;
}
.div-2 {
  width: 60px;
  height: 170px;
  background-color: blue;
  font-size: 24px;
  flex-grow: 1;
}


.div-3 {
  width: 100px;
  height: 180px;
  background-color: green;
  font-size: 24px;
}
.div-4 {
  width: 180px;
  height: auto;
  background-color: mediumspringgreen;
}
.div-5 {
  width: 240px;
  height: auto;
  background-color: orangered;
```

```
      }
</style>
<div class="wrapper">
  <div class="div-1">1</div>
  <div class="div-2">2</div>
  <div class="div-3">3</div>
  <div class="div-4">

    Lorem ipsum dolor sit, amet consectetur
adipisicing elit.
  </div>
  <div class="div-5">

    Lorem ipsum dolor sit amet consectetur
adipisicing elit. Dolores, debitis
    necessitatibus. Nesciunt sequi
reprehenderit dolorum?
  </div>
</div>
```

grow .div-3

Now I will also let the green div .div-3 grow

```
.div-3 {
  width: 100px;
  height: 180px;
  background-color: green;
  font-size: 24px;
  flex-grow: 1;
}
```

You can determine how much everyone should grow. I will give the blue div a value of 3

```css
.div-2 {
  width: 60px;
  height: 170px;
  background-color: blue;
  font-size: 24px;
  flex-grow: 3;
}
.div-3 {
  width: 100px;
  height: 180px;
  background-color: green;
  font-size: 24px;
  flex-grow: 1;
}
```

flex-shrink

The flex-shrink property determines how the element shrinks in relation to the other flexible elements in the same container.

Values

- number

number

Update .div-2 so that it shrinks 4x more than other elements.

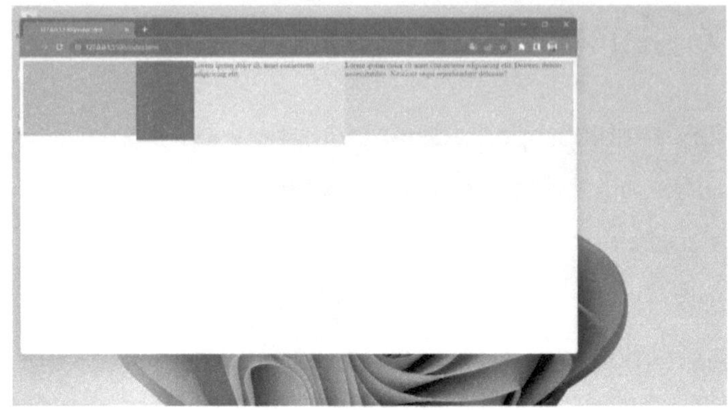

```
<style>
  .wrapper {
    display: flex;
    flex-direction: row;
    flex-wrap: nowrap;
  }
  .div-1 {
    width: 300px;
    height: 160px;
    background-color: magenta;
  }
  .div-2 {
    width: 500px;
    height: 170px;
    background-color: blue;
    flex-shrink: 4;
  }
```

```css
    .div-3 {
      width: 400px;
      height: 180px;
      background-color: lightpink;
    }
    .div-4 {
      width: 600px;
      height: 160px;
      background-color: orange;
    }
```
</style>
<div class="wrapper">
  <div class="div-1"></div>
  <div class="div-2"></div>
  <div class="div-3">
    Lorem ipsum dolor sit, amet consectetur
adipisicing elit.
  </div>
  <div class="div-4">
    Lorem ipsum dolor sit amet consectetur
adipisicing elit. Dolores, debitis
    necessitatibus. Nesciunt sequi
reprehenderit dolorum?
  </div>
</div>

prevent shrink

To prevent an element from shrinking, set its value to 0.

flex-shrink: 0

I will prevent the first div element from shrinking

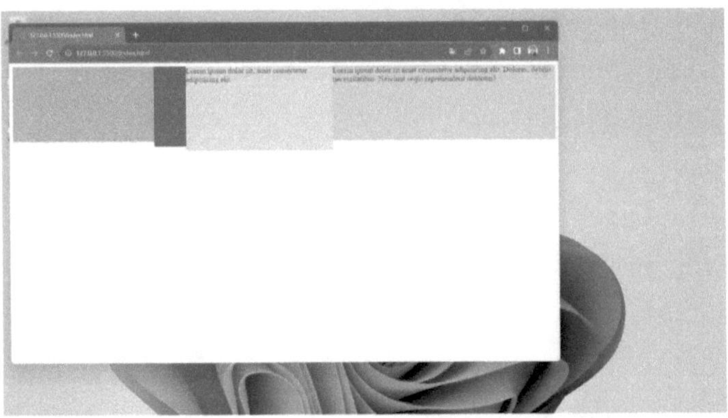

```
.div-1 {
  width: 300px;
  height: 160px;
  background-color: magenta;
```

```
    flex-shrink: 0;
}
```

flex-basis

The flex-basis property defines the initial length of a flex
element.flex-basis has a higher priority than width or
height (if set).
Values

- auto
- number

auto

Default value. The length is equal to the length of the
flexible item. If the item has no length specified, the
length will be according to its content.

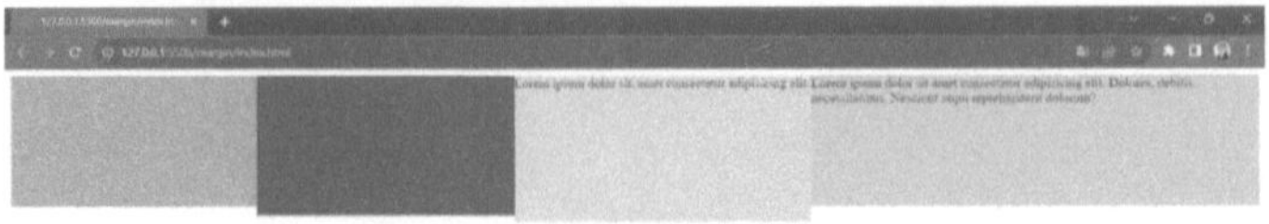

```css
.div-1 {
  width: 300px;
  height: 160px;
  background-color: magenta;
  flex-shrink: 0;
  flex-basis: auto;
}
```

number

A length unit, or percentage, specifying the initial length
of the flexible item(s)

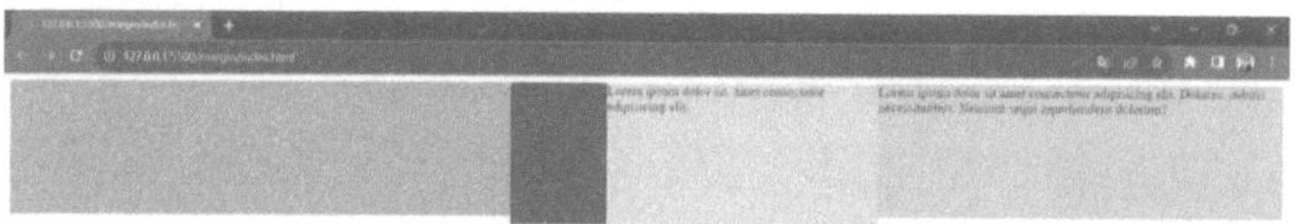

```css
.div-1 {
  width: 300px;
  height: 160px;
  background-color: magenta;
  flex-shrink: 0;
  flex-basis: 600px;
}
```

flex

The flex property is a shorthand property for:

flex: <flex-grow>< flex-shrink> <flex-basis>

Values

- flex-grow flex-shrink flex-basis
- auto
- none

flex-grow flex-shrink flex-basis

Initial value is

flex: 0 1 auto

One value

1. <flex-grow>. In the case of a value, this is assigned to the <flex-grow>.
2. <flex-basis>. If it is not a valid value for the <flex-grow>, it is assigned to the <flex-basis>

Two values

1. <flex-grow>. The first value must be a valid value for the <flex-grow> while the second value is assigned first to <flex-shrink> if possible.
2. <flex-basis>. Otherwise it will be assigned to <flex-basis>

Three values

1. <flex-grow> <flex-shrink> <flex-basis>.

order

The order property specifies the order of a flexible item relative to the rest of the flexible items inside the same container.

The elements are arranged visually according to their order number, lowest values first.

Values

- number

It's not only about ordering elements, but also about grouping elements.

You can use the order property to group elements.

Here is an example, we have some div elements like this:

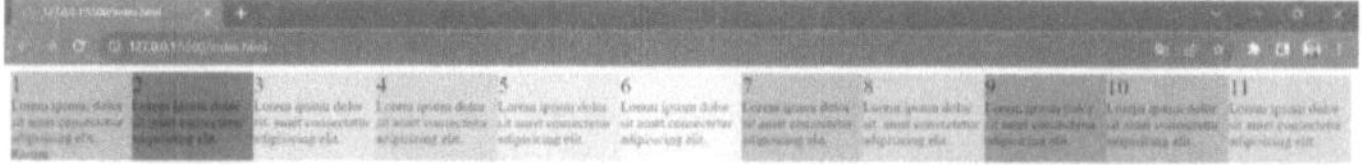

```
<style>
```

```css
.wrapper {
  display: flex;
  flex-direction: row;
  flex-wrap: nowrap;
}
.wrapper div {
  width: 160px;
  height: 100px;
}
.wrapper div span {
  display: block;
  font-size: 25px;
}
.div-1 {
  background-color: magenta;
}
.div-2 {
  background-color: blue;
}
.div-3 {
  background-color: lightpink;
}
.div-4 {
  background-color: orange;
}
.div-5 {
```

```css
    background-color: lightgreen;
  }
  .div-6 {
    background-color: antiquewhite;
  }
  .div-7 {
    background-color: cornflowerblue;
  }
  .div-8 {
    background-color: darkturquoise;
  }
  .div-9 {
    background-color: darkorchid;
  }
  .div-10 {
    background-color: mediumpurple;
  }
  .div-11 {
    background-color: sandybrown;
  }
</style>
<div class="wrapper">
  <div class="div-1">
    <span>1</span>
    Lorem ipsum, dolor sit amet consectetur
adipisicing elit. Rerum.
```

```html
    </div>
    <div class="div-2">
      <span>2</span>
      Lorem ipsum dolor sit amet consectetur
adipisicing elit.
    </div>
    <div class="div-3">
      <span>3</span>
      Lorem ipsum dolor sit, amet consectetur
adipisicing elit.
    </div>
    <div class="div-4">
      <span>4</span>
      Lorem ipsum dolor sit amet consectetur
adipisicing elit.
    </div>
    <div class="div-5">
      <span>5</span>
      Lorem ipsum dolor sit amet consectetur
adipisicing elit.
    </div>
    <div class="div-6">
      <span>6</span>
      Lorem ipsum dolor sit amet consectetur
adipisicing elit.
    </div>
```

```html
<div class="div-7">
  <span>7</span>
  Lorem ipsum dolor sit amet consectetur
adipisicing elit.
  </div>
  <div class="div-8">
  <span>8</span>
  Lorem ipsum dolor sit, amet consectetur
adipisicing elit.
  </div>
  <div class="div-9">
  <span>9</span>
  Lorem ipsum dolor sit amet consectetur
adipisicing elit.
  </div>
  <div class="div-10">
  <span>10</span>
  Lorem ipsum dolor sit amet consectetur
adipisicing elit.
  </div>
  <div class="div-11">
  <span>11</span>
  Lorem ipsum dolor sit amet consectetur
adipisicing elit.
  </div>
</div>
```

number

Now, let's group 6 and 7 together.

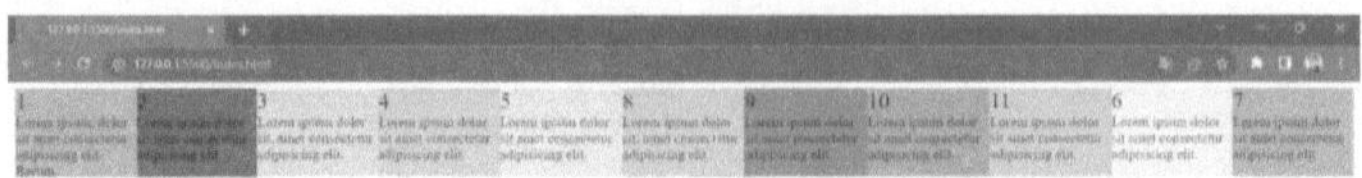

```css
.div-6 {
  background-color: antiquewhite;
  order: 1;
}
.div-7 {
  background-color: cornflowerblue;
  order: 1;
}
```

negative number

Flex items have a default order value of 0.

Now set order to -1;

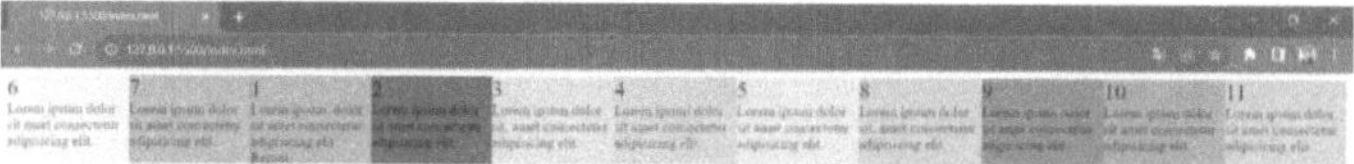

```css
.div-6 {
  background-color: antiquewhite;
  order: -1;
}
.div-7 {
  background-color: cornflowerblue;
  order: -1;
}
```

You can group and order elements using the flex order property

Note that the order property, like all flex properties, only works for flex layouts. If the element is not a flexible element, the order property has no effect.

The last property we are going to discuss here is the align-self.

align-self

The CSS property align-self overrides the value align-items of a flex element.

The align-self property is set per element in order to apply an alignment that differs from the alignment of the container for all elements.

It accepts the same values as align-items, but again, it only works for the element, not the container.

Values

- auto
- stretch
- center
- flex-start
- flex-end
- baseline

Here is an example. We have many div elements inside a container that has align-items: flex-end;

Now, I will apply align-self to .div-5 and .div-6

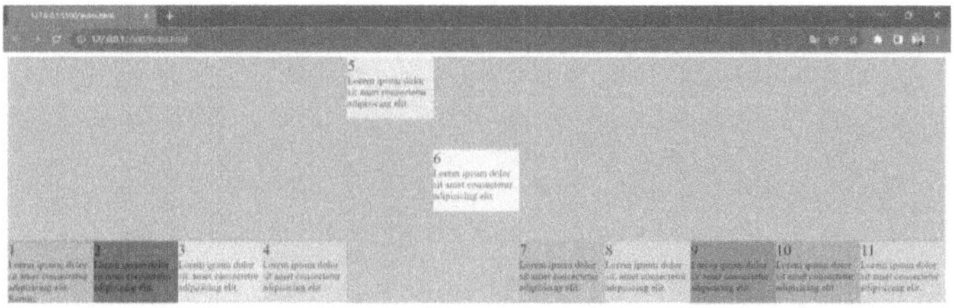

```html
<style>
  .wrapper {
    display: flex;
    flex-direction: row;
    flex-wrap: nowrap;
    height: 400px;
    background-color: lightseagreen;
    align-items: flex-end;
  }
  .wrapper div {
    width: 160px;
    height: 100px;
  }
  .wrapper div span {
    display: block;
    font-size: 25px;
  }
```

```css
.div-1 {
  background-color: magenta;
}
.div-2 {
  background-color: blue;
}
.div-3 {
  background-color: lightpink;
}
.div-4 {
  background-color: orange;
}
.div-5 {
  background-color: lightgreen;
  align-self: flex-start;
}
.div-6 {
  background-color: antiquewhite;
  align-self: center;
}
.div-7 {
  background-color: cornflowerblue;
}
.div-8 {
  background-color: darkturquoise;
}
```

```css
    .div-9 {
      background-color: darkorchid;
    }
    .div-10 {
      background-color: mediumpurple;
    }
    .div-11 {
      background-color: sandybrown;
    }
</style>
<div class="wrapper">
  <div class="div-1">
    <span>1</span>
    Lorem ipsum, dolor sit amet consectetur
adipisicing elit. Rerum.
  </div>
  <div class="div-2">
    <span>2</span>
    Lorem ipsum dolor sit amet consectetur
adipisicing elit.
  </div>
  <div class="div-3">
    <span>3</span>
    Lorem ipsum dolor sit, amet consectetur
adipisicing elit.
  </div>
```

<div class="div-4">
  <span>4</span>
  Lorem ipsum dolor sit amet consectetur adipisicing elit.
</div>
<div class="div-5">
  <span>5</span>
  Lorem ipsum dolor sit amet consectetur adipisicing elit.
</div>
<div class="div-6">
  <span>6</span>
  Lorem ipsum dolor sit amet consectetur adipisicing elit.
</div>
<div class="div-7">
  <span>7</span>
  Lorem ipsum dolor sit amet consectetur adipisicing elit.
</div>
<div class="div-8">
  <span>8</span>
  Lorem ipsum dolor sit, amet consectetur adipisicing elit.
</div>
<div class="div-9">

```html
    <span>9</span>
    Lorem ipsum dolor sit amet consectetur
adipisicing elit.
  </div>
  <div class="div-10">
    <span>10</span>
    Lorem ipsum dolor sit amet consectetur
adipisicing elit.
  </div>
  <div class="div-11">
    <span>11</span>
    Lorem ipsum dolor sit amet consectetur
adipisicing elit.
  </div>
</div>
```

Now we've covered everything to do with the flex layout. By utilizing these features, you can create complex and responsive layouts with ease. I encourage you to experiment and combine different flexbox properties to achieve the layout you want for your website.

Conclusion

Congratulations! You have completed the book "CSS Flexbox Layout". Now you have a comprehensive understanding of the powerful CSS Flexbox system. Remember that learning is an ongoing process. Practice makes perfect — build your own projects, experiment with the features you learn, and delve into the extensive online resources.

Thank you for joining me in my exploration of CSS Flex layout. I wish you the best of luck on your programming journey. Have fun programming and good luck with your applications!

Media Attributions

Modern annual report magazine page flyer a company
catalog
Image by starline on Freepik

Abstract gallery painting
Image by Sketchepedia on Freepik

Don't miss out!

Receive an email when Abdelfattah Ragab publishes a new book. It's free and without obligation.

Also by Abdelfattah Ragab

- ◇ CSS Grid Layout
- ◇ Angular for Beginners
- ◇ Angular Reactive Forms
- ◇ React Portfolio App Development

About the Author

Abdelfattah Ragab is a professional software developer
with more than 20 years of experience.
https://abdelfattah-ragab.com

About the Publisher

Abdelfattah Ragab is a highly qualified and experienced software developer with over 20 years of experience in the industry. Specializing in front-end development, Abdelfattah Ragab has a deep understanding of Angular, JavaScript, TypeScript, HTML and CSS. Read more at https://abdelfattah-ragab.com